The Total Man Series

THE HUMAN SPIRIT

By Dr. Lester Sumrall

Unless otherwise indicated,
all Scripture quotations are taken from
the *King James Version* of the Bible.

The Human Spirit
ISBN 0-937580-33-3
Copyright © 1984 Lester Sumrall
Evangelistic Association
Published by LESEA Publishing Company
P.O. Box 12
South Bend, Indiana 46624

Contents

INTRODUCTION

This is a series of four books packaged together for your convenience. You can also purchase any of the four volumes separately.

This volume describes the unity of the human spirit. It shows how the spirit functions in its relationship in the human personality.

An automobile has 14,000 different parts. When they all perform in unity you have soft and pleasurable transportation.

When your total person is united in oneness with God you are happy, resourceful, and delight in sharing your success with others.

I have been more than twenty years studying the subject of the dividing or separating the human spirit and the human soul. In my search for truth I found little material on the subject. But of recent years there have appeared books and magazine articles on the subject.

It may not be possible to live a victorious and fulfilling life without pertinent knowledge of the total man, spirit, soul, and body.

1

THE SPIRITUAL MAN

A medical doctor once told me that when he was saved and received the Holy Spirit he changed 80% of his prescriptions. He said, "Before I was saved I was a mechanical doctor. I had learned certain methods in medical school and I gave advice and prescriptions according to my learning. When God's Spirit came into me, I saw humans like God sees them. I knew their needs, not from a medical sense, but from a spiritual sense. Many times I said, 'You know, you don't need any medicine. I'll give you a prayer for free and that's all you need.' I would pray for them and they would go on their way."

INTUITION COMES FROM GOD

Your spirit being is made up of a composite of several things.

Through your spirit you can know evil that
nobody else knows anything about. You have
intuition, you can meet a person and know
more about him than the person knows about
himself. By steadily looking at him, God
begins to speak through your spirit about that
person. You know evil and goodness just by
coming into its presence. That intuition works
in spiritual things. You begin to know God in
a way that others do not know Him. To the
sinner, God is a great big man upstairs. To
you, He is not a man and He is not upstairs.
To you, He is right down on the inside of you.

Intuition is one of the great propensities of
the spirit man within you. You must release it,
you must let it go, and not inhibit it. God
wants a free flow of the personality. All babies
are born that way; when they come into the
world, they are born with a free personality.
When the spirit of man comes alive, a power
of intuition begins to look into things
and show you things that other people
do not see. I believe we can know things in
politics that others would not know. Christians really have an advantage over everybody
they meet, but you must talk slowly enough
to let God do it through you. You have a
power there called understanding. You will
understand people's feelings that others will

not understand. Others might hurt a person but you will not hurt him because you have a feeling for him. You have intuition toward human life. The greatest place to release this is toward God. It gives you an insight into God. It gives you a revelation of God through the born-again spirit.

The next area of the spirit is communion. Your spirit is your center of communion, not your brain. You may try to have communion with God through your brain but you will not get very far. God does not respond to your brain. The Bible says, "By wisdom men knew not God." You do not come to know God through man's earthly wisdom. You come to know God by faith and the confession of your sin. Communion comes from the spirit part of you. Many people do not release this part of their spirit life. You can have communion with God at any time, He is there all the time. Communion goes further than God; it goes toward man. Christians are the sweetest people in the world to be around. They are the nicest folk on the face of this earth. God makes the difference.

YOUR CONSCIENCE

Another area of the spirit is conscience. Why can sinners do so many things that are bad and keep what we call a good conscience?

When I was deep in China I kept studying the Chinese people all the time. As we were on the road going up to Tibet, I would ask them questions. I asked a man, "Is it wrong to steal?" I guess he had been guilty, because he looked around cautiously before answering me. I said, "Come on now, this is just between friends. Is it wrong to steal?" "Well," he finally responded, "I'll tell you. If nobody finds it out, it's all right. But if somebody finds out, it's really bad to steal." Then I backed up a little and retorted, "Now, you mean that doing it is not bad in itself?" He did not know what to say. "Well," his answer came, "you see, it is not embarrassing unless someone finds out." I said, "I'm not talking about embarrassment, I'm talking about God. You believe in a god, and you know what is good and what is bad." "Well," he rebuffed, "it is all right to do it if you don't get caught. That's all I know." I said, "No, that is not right. You should not do it if it is wrong. If it is bad, it is bad. It is never good if it is bad. You have to have a conscience in you." Part of your spirit is your conscience. Your conscience can grow.

Many years ago I was sitting down with a

newspaper in my hand, reading the comics. A woman passed by and said, "Are you a Christian?" I replied, "Yes." She quipped, "It doesn't look like it." I can't stand the comics to this day! Nobody, my wife or anyone else, has ever seen me read them. Why? My spirit came alive within me. My spirit, my conscience part of me, said, "I'm bigger and better than that junk. I don't have to put that into my mind." Your conscience is different from other people's conscience. A born-again person has a different idea about the whole of life than anybody else through his conscience that God has given him.

Sometimes people have what we call a seared conscience. It is burned out, worn out, and not used. However, whatever was wrong when you first got saved is still wrong. I have heard people say, "You know when I first got saved I could not do this or that or the other thing, but I can do it all right now." That means they began in the Spirit, like the book of Galatians says, and ended in the flesh. God wants us to live by our spirit. Your spirit is the king of your life! It must direct everything that is done. The boss does not come from the feelings and thinking of your soul. The authority comes from what God has planted on the inside of us through the Holy Spirit.

PUT CHRIST ON THE THRONE
OF YOUR LIFE

We must live, walk, pray, sing, and reign with Christ in the spirit. Then we become more than conquerors in the spirit. We have no condemnation, guilt, worry, or fear in our spirits. Our spirit will then take the royal nature upon itself.

Revelation 1:6, "And hath made us kings and priests unto God and his Father; to him be glory and dominion for ever and ever." We have been made kings and priests in our spiritual parts, not in our soulical parts. We are not the same as a king on the throne in Europe. We are kings and priests in our spiritual realm. We rule spiritually.

The priest heals and the king bosses. When your spirit becomes king of your life and dominates your total personality, and the priestly nature flows through you to serve the whole personality, then your spirit is the king of your life, your soul is the servant of your life, and your body is the slave of your life. If you do not keep them that way, you will never flow in the Spirit of God.

The Greek word "pneuma" means spirit, the human spirit. The Greek word "psuche" defines the human soul. Your human being is not naturally dirty. If it is bad, it is because the devil made it bad. The soul is not spiritual, but it is not dirty. It is what you make it to be as you grow up. In your soulish part, you have your intellectual being.

LIFE FLOWS OUT OF OUR BELLIES

We have within us a kingly spirit that rules the rest of our total personality. Your appetite cannot tell you how much to eat. Your spirit tells you how much to eat. If you do not function that way, you will be out of the Spirit of God. Proverbs 20:27 says, "The spirit of man is the candle of the LORD, searching all the inward parts of the belly." Christ said, "Out of his belly shall flow rivers of living water." That is the way I discovered where a man's spirit is. God taught me that you have two thrones inside of you. You have a throne over your soulical being in the mind and a throne in your belly over the spiritual man.

Jesus said, John 7:38, ". . .out of his belly shall flow rivers of living water." Jesus has to be the king. The spirit-man has to be in charge and if your Adamic nature becomes the king, you will not live a victorious life. Of all the people I meet, possibly 90% of the Christians still live in their soulish nature. This is especially true in the area of their intellect and emotions. If you are going to live in the area of your emotions, and be controlled by them, you will be like a little leaf on the water, constantly tossed back and forth.

2

THE BIRTH OF
THE HUMAN SPIRIT

What is the birth of the human spirit? The Lord Jesus Christ gave us the finest definition of it in John 3:3, "Jesus answered and said unto him, Verily, verily, I say unto thee, Except a man be born again, he cannot see the kingdom of God." That is one of the strongest statements in the Bible. Until this new birth comes and this third person moves inside of you, you cannot experience the kingdom of God. You are on the outside of God. You only come to the inward parts of God when you have experienced what Jesus called a "born-again" experience.

WHAT DOES "BORN AGAIN" MEAN?

John 3:4 says, "Nicodemus saith unto

him, How can a man be born when he is old? can he enter the second time into his mother's womb, and be born?" We understand that at that time Nicodemus could possibly have been 90 years old. His mother probably was dead. He was wondering how he was going to get born again. How could he enter a second time into his mother's womb and be born? This was a wise man and one of the members of the Supreme Court that was talking.

Verse 5, "Jesus answered, Verily, verily, I say unto thee, Except a man be born of water and of the Spirit, he cannot enter into the kingdom of God." What did Jesus mean here? He meant that when you are born of the water it is a public testimony that you have come unto God. It testifies that you have died to the things of the world, the flesh, and it announces that you have come alive unto God. When you are born with a public witness, you are known by the blood of the Lamb and the word of your testimony. Water baptism is a word of testimony that we have truly been born again. So you have to be born of the water and of the Spirit. Unless you have done that you cannot enter into the kingdom of God.

Verse 6, "That which is born of the flesh is

flesh; and that which is born of the Spirit is spirit.''

Verse 7, ''Marvel not that I said unto thee, Ye must be born again.''

A NEW HEART

When a child is born into this world, according to what Jesus said, the spirit element in him is dead because of his Adamic nature. We read in the book of Ezekiel 36:26-27, ''A new heart also will I give you, and a new spirit will I put within you: and I will take away the stony heart out of your flesh, and I will give you an heart of flesh. And I will put my spirit within you, and cause you to walk in my statutes, and ye shall keep my judgments, and do them.'' This is not the carnal man, neither is it the natural man. This is not the way a child grows up because a child by nature is a sinner and a transgressor. A child will not normally tell the truth when it is convenient for him to lie, and he will take that which does not belong to him. When that new heart and new spirit come within him, he will walk in God's statutes and keep His commandments. These are two evidences that he has been born of the spirit and that a new person has emerged. How else can a man fulfill God's plan for his life? There is no other way. You can do anything else that you wish; yet, you cannot perform what God wants you to perform without the new birth. The birth of the Spirit in our lives is the greatest and most important event that can possibly take place in the life of a human.

THE SPIRIT OF LIFE

We read in Romans 8:10, "And if Christ be in you, the body is dead because of sin; but the Spirit is life because of righteousness." When you come to the Lord Jesus Christ and are born again, the old ways and desires are dead, gone, and finished. Instead, there is a spirit of life that brings about righteousness and causes you to walk, talk, and think right. The coming of God's Spirit into our spirit does something amazing for us.

Paul said further in Romans 8:11, "But if the Spirit of him that raised up Jesus from the dead dwell in you, he that raised up Christ from the dead shall also quicken your mortal bodies by his Spirit that dwelleth in you." The word "quicken" is an old English word that means that something is not dead; rather, it is alive, it moves, and it shakes.

An example of this could be in the life of Noah. When Noah had gone through the flood and had been in that awful ark for about a year and finally the rains and the floods had stopped, he wanted to come out of that ark. He let a dove out through the upper window to see if she could find a lodging place. Genesis 8:8-12, "Also he sent forth a dove from him, to see if the waters were abated from off the face of the ground; but the dove found no rest for the sole of her foot, and she returned unto him into the ark, for the waters were on the face of the whole earth: then he put forth his hand, and took her, and pulled her in unto him into the ark. And he stayed yet other seven days; and again he sent forth the dove out of the ark; And the dove came in to him in the evening; and, lo, in her mouth was an olive leaf plucked off: so Noah knew that the waters were abated from off the earth. And he stayed yet other seven days. . . ."

Seven is God's spiritual number. Then he sent forth the dove which did not return. The dove did not return to the ark because there was a new creation on the face of that earth.

A NEW CREATION IN GOD

God also prepares a place in the Christian for Himself. It is a new creation, not the old creature. God wants us to move into that new creation with Him. He wants us to live with

Him and do the things that belong to the Spirit of God.

If a person is a soulish Christian, then he is essentially what we call a worldly person. Worldly people are sinners and only function in body and soul. Soulish Christians have body, soul, and spirit; however, the human spirit is dormant so that the Christian lives and is motivated by soulical parts. God does not want that. God wants every Christian to be motivated by his spirit. He wants the spirit to be the king of your life. He wants you to obey the movements and operation of the spirit within you.

If you are a genuine Christian and you are active in God through your spirit, you do not live after the soul. Instead, you live after the human spirit that God has placed within you. Then your spirit is fused with God's Spirit and you have a hot line right into the throne room of God.

GOD'S SPIRIT AND MAN'S SPIRIT

In Romans 8, we see how man's spirit becomes one with God's Spirit. In the first seven chapters of Romans the spirit is seldom mentioned, but in Chapter 8 it really comes alive. You can hardly tell the difference between God's Spirit and man's spirit.

Instead of the Adamic soul controlling the spirit, the human spirit now controls the soul and the body.

Romans 8:11 says, "But if the Spirit of him that raised up Jesus from the dead dwell in you, he that raised up Christ from the dead shall also quicken your mortal bodies by his Spirit that dwelleth in you." God through His Spirit dwelling within us wants to command the body and the soul. The big question with so many Christians today is, "How do we function in the spirit and not in the soul? How do you get from moving in the soul to moving in the spirit?" Maybe a testimony would assist us. All of us have heard of the very unusual Christian man named Watchman Nee, the Chinese leader. Watchman Nee said, "We must know that he who can work for God is one whose inward man can be released."

RELEASING THE INWARD MAN

The basic difficulty of a servant of God lies in the failure of the inward man to break through the outward man. God's Spirit that He has placed within you must break through the soulical parts, (your mind, emotions, and will) and the physical five senses (sight, hearing, taste, smell, and touch). If we have never learned how to release our inward man by breaking through the outward man, we are not able to serve the living God as we should. Nothing can so hinder us as the outward man dominating the inward man. When you become born again your soulical part will not be king anymore. He lost his kingship and his preeminence. The inward man becomes the king, the dominant factor in your life. When you pray, you pray by your spirit. When you live, you live by your spirit. Your spirit becomes the real man within you. Christians are different from anybody else on the face of this earth because they are born-again creatures and their lives have been dominated by the Spirit of the living God.

Whether our works are fruitful or not depends upon whether our outward man has been broken by the Lord so that the inward man passes through the brokenness and comes forth. So many times we have to come to the Lord and say, "Lord, break us; break us." What we mean is, "Cause the mind, the emotions, and the willpower to be subservient. Break down the old Adamic nature, the old nature. Let the new life reign and rule in our hearts and lives." Not being broken enough for the spirit man to flow through into the soulical parts could be the basic problem of Christians today. The Lord wants to break our outward man in order that the inward man may have its expression to the world in the outward area. When the inward man is released and the spirit begins to flow out, non-believers and Christians alike will be blessed. Everybody around us will be blessed because the inward man always brings blessing.

MOVING TO A HIGHER PLANE

You are working on a higher plane when you are living by your spirit. You are still using your soul when your spirit uses your mind, but your spirit is the dominant factor. The spirit knows more because it relates to both worlds. It is related to God and knows the mind of God, and at the same time it knows what is best for the natural man. It is a double blessing when the spirit rules the life.

Man was not supposed to eat of the Tree of the Knowledge of Good and Evil. God said it, but man disobeyed. This happened while Adam and Eve lived in the garden of Eden. The soul then became over-developed. The Tree of Life would have been for the development of the spirit, but Adam and Eve never got to that tree. All they had was the Tree of Knowledge of Good and Evil, which is related to the development of the soul. In the eternal life we are going to have the development of the spirit; we will be eating of the Tree of Life, not just the Tree of the Knowledge of Good and Evil.

WHAT IS MAN'S BASIC PROBLEM?

The over-development of the soul or the inordinate affection of the soul has long been considered by great Christians as man's basic problem. If we are going to take the mind, emotions, and the will and let them be kings in our life, we are going to be up and down and in and out. If we do not work on a higher level, we will not be what God wants us to be. The soul can do many things. It can even put a man on the moon. However, it is utterly helpless in the things of the spirit. The soul cannot perform the works of the spirit. Your mind, emotions, and will absolutely cannot reach up and magnify God and praise God like He wants to be praised. He wants the spirit of man to do that.

We have an example in the Old Testament. When the children of Israel wished to offer themselves in full sacrifice to Jehovah, they did so by bringing a little pigeon, or a dove, or a lamb as a sacrifice. This little animal or bird was to act as their personal sacrifice. The first thing the high priest did was to take a sharp knife and cut the offering into small pieces before the Lord. In the New Testament period, we do not bring doves, pigeons, and lambs to church. The real surrender, the real offering, is within us. We must bring ourselves in full surrender. Even today, the procedure is the same.

A SWORD TO DIVIDE

Jesus Christ, our high priest, takes a sharper knife than any Old Testament high priest ever had and He divides the spirit and the soul. The Word of God is living and powerful. The Word of God is sharper than any two-edged sword; it pierces to the dividing asunder of soul and spirit. The Bible is the sharp sword that can discern and say, "Wait a minute; this is spirit and this is soul. This is living by God and this is living by Adam." Only the Word of God can teach us and show us exactly which is which.

Man is made in the image and likeness of God; he is tripartite: spirit, soul, and body. His soul is also tripartite: will, mind, and emotions. Try as you may, you will not find a fourth compartment of the soul. In the spirit we are also divided into three compartments: intuition (knowing without thinking it out as the intellect has to do in the soulical parts), communion (fellowship with the Father and

His Son, the Lord Jesus Christ, which you cannot have without the born-again experience and your spirit coming alive), and conscience (inner witness to the Word of God). The body and the soul are subject to death because of sin, but the spirit is the substance of God.

THE FATHER OF SPIRITS

Hebrews 12:9 says, "We have had fathers of our flesh which corrected us, and we gave them reverence: shall we not much rather be in subjection unto the Father of spirits, and live." God is the Father of spirits. The spirit in the unregenerated human is dead, or alienated from God. It is inactive, but that does not mean that it is extinct. The spirit, once renewed, is alive. It is clothed with a soul and a body, which become the media of expression for the spirit. The natural man is manifested and sustained in this life by his body. A sick body can destroy the manifestation of the mind; it can destroy the emotions; it can destroy the will. The human spirit enters reality only through the soul and body; likewise the spirit exits the body by natural death or sin. The impartation of eternal life is through the ingrafted seed of the Lord Jesus Christ. James 1:21 says it this way, "Wherefore lay apart all filthiness and superfluity of naughtiness, and receive with meekness the engrafted word, which is able to save your souls." I Peter 1:23 says, "Being born again, not of corruptible seed, but of incorruptible, by the word of God, which liveth and abideth for ever."

Our conscience is spirit, by it we know the laws of God. The spirit then dictates the law of God to the soul, which enforces that law. The modern world is void of pure conscience; instead, it lives by the soulish mental powers, or methods. The soul looks for numbers to count; the spirit looks for holiness, meekness, joy, etc.

GOD NEEDS YOU— SPIRIT, SOUL, AND BODY

There are three main words that describe the nature of man: his spirit, his soul, and his body. Now God needs all three of them. Man, through his body, can contact the outward world; through his bodily senses he is world-conscious. Man, through his soul, is able to know himself; he is what we call self-conscious. In his spirit area, man has the capacity to know God; he possesses the capacity to be God-conscious. The three elements of the human personality are all needed. Man is like a corporation. When you go into the plant, in the factory you see the assembly room where the people are putting the products together. This is comparable to the human body. In the office, you see the secretaries and the assistants working. This is comparable to the human soul. When you go into the president's office, you find the source of all the truth, the life, and the vision of the company. This is comparable to the human spirit. In the fallen man the governing office has been taken from the spirit and transferred to the soul of man; that is the fallen, sinful man. When the man comes back to God, he discovers a new world, a new life, and a new power.

Psalm 34:18, "The LORD is nigh unto them that are of a broken heart." The spirit ought to be ruling the center of our personality, and whenever God does not rule in man's spirit, the spiritual personality lies dormant and is not productive and does not produce a glorious, happy, fruitful Christian.

3

LIFE IN THE SPIRIT

If the soul becomes the king and the ruler, it will destroy what the spirit builds. The soul must be broken before the spirit can be released and flow through a person's soul and body.

The Holy Spirit comes from God and communicates with the human spirit. Besides Jesus, Adam was the fullest expression of the human spirit ever on the face of this earth. When Adam rebelled and disobeyed God, his spirit died. It ceased its relationship with God the Father. His actions and thoughts were now controlled by a body and by soulical parts. Then Satan began to control his personality.

That which perished in Adam was resurrected in Christ! We call that the "new birth."

There are four words for "life" in the Greek language. One is "Bios," the lowest form of life. There is "Psuche," the soulical area. "Zoe" is the spiritual life, the Christ-life, the God-life, eternal life. This "Zoe" life is what John speaks of in I John 5:11-12, "And this is the record, that God hath given to us eternal life, and this life is in his Son. He that hath the Son hath life; and he that hath not the Son of God hath not life." The fourth of these is the "Anastrophe," a confused manner of behavior used only once in the Scriptures.

THE "ZOE" LIFE

In Christ we receive the "Zoe," the spiritual life, the divine nature. What we call the spirit of man inside of him is that "Zoe" life. The spirit of man is his born-again experience.

John 3:16 says, "For God so loved the world that he gave his only begotten Son, that whosoever believeth in him should not perish, but have everlasting life." This speaks of the fusing of man's spirit with God's Spirit. The word "world" is one of those beautiful words that can mean the cosmos, or it can mean the geographical earth, or it can mean the people. It is the people that God loved. God loved the people so much that He gave His only begotten Son so that whosoever believed in Him would not perish. God wanted people to have life, the fusing of man's spirit with God's spirit. Ephesians 2:1 says, "And you hath he quickened, who were dead in trespasses and sins." The anointing is when God's Spirit possesses the human spirit and that spirit becomes renewed.

Ephesians 4:23 urges us to, ". . .be renewed in the spirit of your mind." This renewing must come out of your spirit and flow into your soulical parts. When this happens, your mind is cleansed by the blood of Jesus.

Ezekiel calls it a new spirit. Ezekiel 18:31, "Cast away from you all your transgressions, whereby ye have transgressed; and make you a new heart and a new spirit: for why will ye die?" God wants us to have that new spirit. This is the "Zoe" life, the spiritual life, God's life.

In the Bible when a man received this new spirit, he would never again deal with men in his Adamic nature. Paul said he knew no man by the flesh.

WHAT IS IN A NAME?

In my travels around the country I have heard people speak of the other people saying, "Oh, what do you mean, old Fatso?"

You cannot know that man by the size of his body. Inside of him might be a mountain of strength and a mountain of God's might. His spirit might be tremendously alive. So you must not know him after the flesh and call him "Fatso." We should know him by "Zoe," by his spirit, by God's Spirit dwelling within that man. I want to urge you not to call people by slang names.

· We have a striking example in the man Jacob. "Jacob" was his soulical name. The name Jacob means "a person that takes from another." He was one for grabbing something that was not his. The word Israel means "A prince with God."

During Jacob's soulical times people called him Jacob. When he had his amazing conversion experience and was born again, the Spirit of God moved upon him and the angel of God blessed him. The angel said, "You are no longer Jacob, you are Israel." After that people could not know him by his body, because his body was crippled. The angel hit him and he forever dragged one leg behind him. People could have gone around saying, "There goes old Crip," but they would have missed him altogether. Inside he was 10 feet tall.

I lived in China for a long time and they

had a most interesting practice. They had secret nicknames for the missionaries. They would say, "Over in that missionary's home, the servant girl calls the mistress 'Tiger' in Chinese." The woman does not understand Chinese so she does not know that she is being called "Tiger." The names were picked because of the missionaries' personalities. We do not want to know people after their soulical parts. We want to know people by their spiritual beings. We want to know if they are strong in faith and big in love.

Ishmael was a son of the flesh. Galatians 4:23 says that he was of the bondwoman and that he was born after the flesh. This son of the flesh was a thorn in the side of Abraham as long as he lived. II Corinthians 10:3 says, "For though we walk in the flesh, we do not war after the flesh." Though we are related to the flesh, it is not a god or a king, or a ruler; it is under subjection to the "Zoe" life that comes from God.

Very often when you come to God, He gives you another name. The Lord Jesus encountered Peter and said, "I'll change your name. You were Simon; you are now Peter; you are a rock. Jacob's name was changed from "Supplanter" to "Prince of God."

Nowhere in the Bible do you have a

description of the physical parts of Jesus. Matthew probably wanted to write down, "He stood 6 feet 2 inches, and his eyes were flaming and dark brown, the curves around His mouth were so strong," but the Holy Spirit said, "Rub it out; rub it out." God was determined that we should only know Him by His spirit and not His body. He did not come for us to worship His body; He came for us to worship His spirit. We are not to be like Him in our bodies; we are to be like Him in our spirits.

THE VICTORIOUS CHRISTIAN ENERGIZED BY GOD'S SPIRIT

The human spirit must be related to the glorious kingdom of God upon this earth. I could not give a definition for the spirit until God gave me Romans 14:17, "The kingdom of God is... righteousness, and peace, and joy." We have the righteousness, peace, and joy of the kingdom. Isaiah said in Isaiah 12:3, "Therefore with joy shall ye draw water out of the wells of salvation." I Peter 1:8 says, "Whom having not seen, ye love; in whom, though now ye see him not, yet believing, ye rejoice with joy unspeakable and full of glory." That is your spirit. The human personality becomes a dwelling place of the Most

High God. Man has only his spirit to deal with in the great issues of life. God wants your spirit renewed within you and strengthened within you. Your spirit must grow stronger and stronger every day.

When I knew Smith Wigglesworth, he was 85 years old. Although his body could not run a race, his spirit could rise up like a giant within him. How glorious it was that his spirit was not getting weak with his body. He talked with such faith, such strength, such power, and such vitality, even at 85 years of age.

Numbers 14:24 tells us the secret of another 85-year old man who took an entire mountain single-handedly. "But my servant Caleb, because he had another spirit with him, and hath followed me fully, him will I bring into the land whereinto he went; and his seed shall possess it."

Joshua 14:6-13, "Then the children of Judah came unto Joshua in Gilgal: and Caleb the son of Jephunneh the Kenezite said unto him, Thou knowest the thing that the LORD said unto Moses the man of God concerning me and thee in Kadesh-barnea. Forty years old was I when Moses the servant of the LORD sent me from Kadesh-barnea to espy out the land; and I brought him word again as it was in mine heart. Nevertheless my brethren that went up with me made the heart of the people melt: but I wholly followed the LORD my God. And Moses sware on that day, saying, Surely the land whereon thy feet have trodden shall be thine inheritance, and thy children's for ever, because thou hast wholly followed the LORD my God. And now, behold, the LORD hath kept me alive, as he said, these forty and five years, even since the LORD spake this word unto Moses, while the children of Israel wandered in the wilderness: and now, lo, I am this day fourscore and five years old. As yet I am as strong this day as I was in the day that Moses sent me: as my strength then, even so is my strength now, for war, both to go out, and to come in. Now therefore give me this mountain, whereof the LORD spake in that day; for thou heardest in that day how the Anakims were there, and that the cities were great and fenced: if so be the LORD will be with me, then I shall be able to drive them out, as the LORD said. And Joshua blessed him, and gave unto Caleb the son of Jephunneh Hebron for an inheritance.

Caleb was a victor because of the spirit within him.

4

HOW THE SPIRIT-MAN OPERATES

Job 32:8 says, "There is a spirit in man: and the inspiration of the Almighty giveth them understanding." The Almighty is the one who gives you your comprehension, understanding, movement, and operation. The Almighty is interested in your spirit. He directs, helps, and blesses in your spirit area.

YOUR SPIRIT HAS ITS OWN PERSONALITY

We read in Zechariah 12:1, "The burden of the word of the LORD for Israel, saith the LORD, which stretcheth forth the heavens, and layeth the foundation of the earth, and formeth the spirit of man within him." Just as God formed Adam and made him to be a living person, God formed the spirit within you. Your spirit has personality that nobody else has. You are an individual. You are as different from every other spirit as each snowflake is different from every other snowflake, or as every fingerprint is different from every other fingerprint. God is inexhaustible in His expression. Your spirit is related to God in the way that you yield to God, making you different from any other person that ever lived.

There are over 4 billion people living on the face of the earth right now. Everyone of those persons is different. There are no two identical humans. Your spirit that is within you is an individual spirit and no other spirit is like that spirit. Every tender touch of God makes you different from somebody else.

God forms the spirit that is within us by our reactions to His movings in our lives. Proverbs 20:27 says, "The spirit of man is the candle of the LORD, searching all the inward parts of the belly." God says your spirit is the light of the Lord on this earth. Sinners do not have this.

We must arrive at a place where our inner impulses and our inner emotions follow the living Spirit of God and not the Adamic nature. Our spirits are the candle of God on the face of the earth. We are the light of heaven. It is not your soul, mind, emotions, or your will, but the newborn thing within you that is the candle of God. When you are born again, you become God's candle to light up the earth. Matthew 5:14, "Ye are the light of the world. A city that is set on an hill cannot be hid." The headquarters and the throne room of this new personality is in the cavity of the belly of your body. Somebody must sit on the throne; either God sits upon the throne or the devil sits on it.

James 2:26 says, "For as the body without the spirit is dead. . ." It is spiritually dead. "Death" has many definitions; it does not always mean extinction. The father said of his prodigal son, "This is my son that was dead." He was not off the face of the earth; he was separated from the father. So death can also mean separation. God is telling us here that the body without the spirit is inactive, it is not functioning. God said the spirit of man has to keep moving and living so that the rest of our personality can function in God.

POWER WITH GOD IS IN THE ANOINTING

I once knew an evangelist who had little or

no education. He spoke the king's English backward, sideways, and a few other ways, but when he ministered under the anointing of God, cancers would disappear before your eyes. When I had a lump underneath my eye that would not go away, he prayed for it and in a second it was gone and never came back. I did not care what kind of English he spoke; that had nothing to do with a lump I could not get rid of. It was his spirit-relation that mattered. If a man looks a little strange, or a little peculiar, or a little backward, test the spirit. We should not judge any man after his height, his wealth, his ingenuity, or functioning of a keen mind; we must know him by one thing, by the breath of the Holy Ghost that flows through him. If you get to knowing people like that, you will have a bushel of friends and people will love you.

WHAT ARE THE ELEMENTS OF THE CHEMISTRY OF THE SPIRIT?

First is revelation. It's a part of the chemistry of the spirit. We use our spirits to receive divine eternal truth from God. For example, in Matthew 16:17, the Lord Jesus Christ turned to Peter and remarked, after the disciple had said in verse 16, "Thou art the Christ, the Son of the living God..." "...Simon

...flesh and blood hath not revealed it unto thee, but my Father which is in heaven."

Your spirit man is your area of receiving spiritual revelation. You cannot receive spiritual revelation through your soulical parts. Many times we try so very hard. We become so proud of our minds. Some people actually worship their minds. Your natural man will always seek to live naturally, but your spiritual man wants to live by revelation. There are people that are born again who cannot discern when the Spirit of God is moving in a meeting, and when it is another spirit. In this revelation aspect we must first know the moving of the Spirit of God.

We must discern ourselves and know when we are moving by God's Spirit, and when we are working with the soulical parts of our Adamic human nature. Many people have a lot more faith than they realize they have. You meet people that are just boiling with faith inside and the devil makes them think they have none. The devil says, "You do not have any faith," yet, he knows they do. The devil never tells the truth. He is a liar and the father of lies. Through the spirit we realize our potential. We learn to believe "I am who God says I am. I can do what God says I can do." You are functioning in your spirit man through revelation. God says it, you believe it, and it works that way! In the chemistry of your spirit, revelation is so important in realizing who you really are, and what your potential is. You cannot really realize it through your brain. You might be able to do a thousand times more than your mind ever tells you you can do.

Not only is the chemistry of your spirit related to revelation, it is very strongly related to what we call conscience. Now the dictionary says that conscience is an inner knowledge of right and wrong. Your conscience generates feelings of guilt if you violate the moral judgment that is within you. Let us look at the Bible for a more accurate definition. Romans 8:16 says, "The Spirit itself beareth witness with our spirit, that we are the children of God." That is your conscience telling you that you are of God, because the Holy Spirit has brought life within your spirit man.

Your conscience can give you direction. Your conscience receives the Word of God and dictates that word to the will, and the will acts upon it. Your conscience can determine a right course or a wrong course, a right thing to do or a wrong thing to do. This direction may not be whether something is sinful or not; it may be in relationship to whether you are acting in God's perfect will or not. If you violate your conscience's direction, you are violating part of your spirit man. If the conscience is telling you what is the best thing to do and you would prefer living your own way, then you have the Adamic nature working within you.

YOUR CONSCIENCE— THE SEAT OF YOUR FAITH

Hebrews 9:14 says, "How much more shall the blood of Christ, who through the eternal Spirit offered himself without spot to God, purge your conscience. . ." God will purge your conscience. Therefore, your conscience is the very seat of your faith. God will purge you of dead things and things that do not produce spirituality. Anything that does not produce spirituality in your life is a dead element. Everything within you that lives is of God. Everything that raises you up higher is of God. These things work through your spirit man, not through your soulical parts, not with your mind, your emotions, your will, and not with your body. They only work through your born-again nature.

I Timothy 1:5, 18, 19 says, "Now the end

of the commandment is charity out of a pure heart, and of a good conscience, and of faith unfeigned. This charge I commit unto thee, son Timothy, according to the prophecies which went before on thee, that thou by them mightest war a good warfare; holding faith, and a good conscience; which some having put away concerning faith have made shipwreck." God wants you, through your conscience, to generate faith in your spiritual man. Your conscience is the center and the heart of your faith. The center is not in your mind, not in your emotions. Faith runs deeper; faith is generated in your spirit part. It flows from that spirit part into your Adamic parts.

5

THE ABUNDANT LIFE

Have you ever picked up the telephone, called a friend, and when you got through to him he said, "I was just going to call you"? That is what you call intuition. You are flowing together. How many times have you been sitting by somebody and suddenly you said something and he said, "I was thinking the same thing"? That is the flowing together of the human spirit.

I Corinthians 2:11, "For what man knoweth the things of a man, save the spirit of man which is in him?. . ." Nobody understands a human being until he knows the human spirit. Psychologists, as long as they believe that man is made of two parts, dualistic, made of mud and air, will never truly understand the human person. If we do not get into the spirit movement, we will never understand truth like we should.

KNOWLEDGE THROUGH REVELATION

There is a part of our spirit man that knows without learning. This is knowledge without reason that comes by the way of revelation. You receive it and you perceive it, but it did not come through your mental faculties; it came through your spirit man. You know it is true and you are sure it is true, but it did not come through your reasoning power.

When I was in Alaska, I knew a man in his 70s who was what we call a "white Russian." He ran away from Russia because of the Communists. He had a shoe repair shop and I would visit with him for long periods of time. One day he looked at me and said, "I want you to tell me something. I was sitting here in this shop praying, thanking God that I was a free man, and suddenly in my spirit I saw a funeral. It was a Russian funeral but I was in Alaska. I looked into the casket and there was my brother. They closed the casket and the funeral guests walked away. I wrote it all down and I wrote to Russia and told what I had seen. My brother's wife wrote back, 'Yes, you saw it, and from your letter you saw it the hour it took place.' " It is remarkable how our spirits within us can move and do such things.

The devil has a counterfeit for everything God does. Just because there are a few $10 bills floating around that are counterfeit, I am not ready to burn real ones. Just because there is a counterfeit, I am not going to downgrade the good. Here was a godly man who had run away from communist Russia because he loved God. The Lord was so kind to him that he awakened something within him in the same hour that his brother was buried; he was at the ceremony by his spirit. There is a place in God where we can have a spiritual faculty. We know that we know. We are sure that we are sure. The power of God is what makes it manifest.

CAN OTHERS PERCEIVE GOD'S SPIRIT IN YOU?

What are some of the divine expressions of the spirit of man within us? We send forth God's spirit to others by our spirit. Sometimes it is received and sometimes it is not. Once I was riding on a big airplane. Normally when I am riding I am working on my studies. I was just sitting there going through my studies, when I glanced across the aisle and there was a woman sticking her tongue out at me. I laughed and she stuck her tongue out again. My spirit was moving around that plane and making her mad. I was not saying a word;

it was just my spirit. She was so full of evil she could not tolerate it. She could not put me off, we were 37,000 feet high, but she could stick her tongue out at me. You can be in the company of some people and they get under conviction of their sin by your very presence! On the other hand, you can heal people. You come into their presence and they say, "I just feel so good with you here."

Galatians 5:22-23 says, "But the fruit of the Spirit is love, joy, peace, longsuffering, gentleness, goodness, faith, meekness, temperance: against such there is no law." So the fruit of the Spirit is expression of the spirit of man. These are the fruit of your human spirit within you, not the fruit of your soulical man. These are the expressions and manifestations of the spirit that was born within you.

The gifts of the Spirit are also in residence in the spirit of man. When God gives you one of the gifts of the Spirit, it becomes resident in your spiritual part. It does not reside in your soulical part: your mind, emotions, or your will, nor the physical part: the five senses, but the spiritual part of you, and flows forth from your spirit. It does not flow through your natural person.

THE HUMAN SPIRIT
SEEKS FELLOWSHIP

What are some of the vital activities of your human spirit? A very beautiful one is fellowship. The human spirit, when it comes alive, seeks and finds relationships with those of like human spirit that they might flow together in the Holy Spirit. This fellowship comes in prayer, song, and praise. In the total human being, man has physical contacts with the earth. Man can have fellowship through soulical contacts with his mind, emotions, and will. Man can also have contact with his spirit. He can flow to another in good things in the Word of God, in song, in the reading of the Word, in prayer, in praise, and so on. This is a great matter of fellowship.

I John 1:7 says, "If we walk in the light, as he is in the light, we have fellowship one with another." One of the activities of the human spirit is fellowship. We have fellowship with each other. Did you know the bonds of Christian fellowship are oftentimes much stronger than the natural bonds of the blood? There are many people who will walk away from kinfolk in order to get over to the church and be with God's people. They say, "Oh, that's where I have my fellowship. We are all brothers and sisters in God, so we are the same family, and have fellowship one with another."

I Corinthians 6:17, "But he that is joined unto the Lord is one spirit." One time in France I was lost and I could not speak French. I had to preach that night, and I did not know how to find the house where I was supposed to stay. Too many houses looked alike, and I could not knock on a thousand house doors. I thought, "Well, all I can do is wander the streets until the police find me. I hope I can find somebody that speaks English." I stood on the street corner and began to pray, "Now Lord, I don't know who I'll ever find in this city that speaks English, and I don't know how I'm going to find my way to church to preach tonight. Lord, you are able to help." At that moment a man on a bicycle came by. He came up very close and said, "Hallelujah!" I said, "Oh, come here! Come here!" I knew "Hallelujah." I said, "I'm going with you." I did not know that he was going to the church where I was to minister!

TRY THE SPIRITS

I John 4:1 says "Beloved, believe not every spirit, but try the spirits whether they are of God." We are living in the days when we need to try spirits and to know what they are saying, and if they are of God or not. Your spirit man is the area of your personality which will reveal this.

Ephesians 5:19, "Speaking to yourselves in psalms, and hymns, and spiritual songs, singing and making melody in your heart to the Lord." The activities of the human spirit are very special and very beautiful.

I Timothy 3:9 says, "Holding the mystery of the faith in a pure conscience." When God takes root in our conscience, He produces these fruits and these tremendous blessings of the Holy Spirit.

Paul says in I Corinthians 14:15, "What is it then? I will pray with the spirit, and I will pray with the understanding also: I will sing with the spirit, and I will sing with the understanding also." We have a right and are commanded to function in our brain and in the spirit.

YOUR SPIRIT SHOULD
RULE SOUL AND BODY

When your natural spirit is born within you and begins to grow up and become a mature Christian within you, it begins to rule and to govern. It identifies the movements in your soul and your body as to whether they are in God or out of God. It also identifies whether your actions are spirit-fulfilling or soul-fulfilling. The spirit begins to utilize the soul and the body for spiritual expression and manifestation.

You can gain strength and power and victory in the workings of your spirit in the areas of unbelief. Many people that have a difficult time believing struggle with trying to believe something. When you are born again you do not have to struggle at all; you just believe. I have no problems at all with believing. I say, "Yeh, sure, sure, bless God. Yes, I believe that. No problem." If you get a spirit of unbelief in you and you will not believe in your brothers and your sisters and will not believe what you hear, eventually you will not even believe the Bible.

In the spirit we can enter an area where we believe God. We can also enter an area where fear and confusion are gone. It is the work of the spirit within us to remove fears, phobias, unbeliefs, and demons. We call it reigning in heavenly places by the spirit.

Your spirit can keep growing. Your spirit is not full-grown the day you are born again. It has just begun to grow and this is a continuing process. When your spirit and soul are right, they go after the body to demand its consecration. That is when your total man functions in harmony with the Most High God.

YOUR SOUL ACTIVITIES REVEAL THE BORN AGAIN SPIRIT IN YOU

Your spirit can keep learning and growing all of your total life. Of course your soulical parts can, too. Your mind will never cease to grow if you will cause it to learn new things every day of its life.

How do we know when we are receiving information from our spirit man or our soulical man? How do you discern the spirit? Maybe this is the biggest of all problems. We know whether we are dealing in the spirit of man or in the soulical parts of man by the source that the information came from. The spoken word reveals what is inside of a person. If the spoken word is coming out of the soulical parts of you, then it is not of the spirit. The spoken word reveals whether or not you are walking in the spirit.

What you desire to read reveals and discerns your spirit. If you enjoy reading novels, shady materials, stories about broken homes, and pornographic literature, you are revealing the spirit inside of you. Your reading material is a discerner of your spirit.

Your choice of companions reveals your spirit. When I got saved there was not a single one of my old companions that wanted to be anywhere around me. If you choose sinful companions, it is a sign you are not walking in the spirit.

Your worship reveals what you are on the inside. Some people only want dead, solemn worship. They think that worship has no relationship to joy, peace, happiness, or the flow of God. Church has to be dead or they cannot stand it. That is because they are dead. It is that simple.

Another indicator of your spirit is your meekness. Your inner person is revealed by whether there is a meek attitude or a stubborn one present in your personality. If you are stubborn, you are not walking in your spiritual man. Meekness and stubbornness in the same person reveals a split between the soul and the spirit.

6

THE SPIRITUAL MAN
IN FINAL BATTLE

The great apostle said in Ephesians 6:10-12, "Finally, my brethren, be strong in the Lord, and in the power of his might. Put on the whole armour of God, that ye may be able to stand against the wiles of the devil. For we wrestle not against flesh and blood, but against principalities, against powers, against the rulers of the darkness of this world, against spiritual wickedness in high places."

We are not wrestling against flesh and blood, or human persons; rather, we are struggling against principalities, areas over which there is an evil prince. We are struggling against powers that are not human; they are above the human. We are struggling against the rulers of the darkness of this world. We are struggling against spiritual wickedness in exalted places, such as politics, religion, and economics. Revelation 12:12 says, "Therefore rejoice, ye heavens, and ye that dwell in them. Woe to the inhabiters of the earth and of the sea! for the devil is come down upon you, having great wrath, because he knoweth that he hath but a short time." There is a final battle in the making. The decisive battle, the final battle is the important one. The one that wins that last battle will have won it all!

THE TIME IS NOW

We are living in the last moments of the generations that live in the Dispensation of Grace. I think we can feel the same as Babylon must have felt in the last night of its history. I believe that people in Babylon were whispering one to another and saying, "There is an eerie feeling in the air." Doomsday was casting its shadows and there were intelligent people that said, "We are getting to the end. Our king is feasting and drinking, but we are at the end of Babylon."

I believe that the citizens of Rome must have felt their doomsday when the firey tongues of hell raced through that imperial city and Rome died. The people must have sensed the impending disaster upon the empire of Rome in its last dying, fiery moments.

Possibly the people in Jerusalem had the same feeling when their capital city was surrounded by the marching legions of imperial Rome. A commandment from the Emperor Titus said, "Burn it to the ground. Destroy it. Don't leave one stone upon another." The citizens of Jerusalem must have felt it!

Today you and I, as Christians, must be sensitive to the return of the Lord Jesus. I believe that we can feel the impending tribulation period as it is approaching the world in which we live.

BE READY

As Christians, you and I must prepare ourselves for the final attack of the enemy upon humanity. According to the Word, the devil is going to fight like a dying animal. He is going to do everything that he possibly can in his last great attack. Man will be at the very center of this final great battle upon the face of this earth. The battle will be in the area of the spirit of man. The spirit of man is the greatest part of man. It is the part of man which has intuition to know God, to love God, and to serve God. It is the part of man that has a conscience with which he gets to know the Most High God, to serve Him, and to worship Him. The final great battle will very strongly be related to the spirit part of the human being.

WHO ARE THE FAITHFUL?

The Lord Jesus said in Luke 18:8, "Will I find faith on the earth when I come?" That means the spirit of man will be attacked. Something will try to destroy the spiritual faith of the human person. However, God's triumphant church will be able to fight the enemy and win in the spirit.

Millions of people will give themselves over to demon worship. The whole of the occult world is an attack on the spirit of man, to steal his spirit away from God. Satan worship, astrology, and the zodiac that have become so popular in our world today are all part of this last great attack on the human spirit.

The battle will be a spiritual battle to destroy the human spirit so that men will not be able to worship or serve God. Satan will come in such deceiving ways that many will not recognize him. His devices may seem so innocent and yet they will trap men's spirits so that they will not be able to worship God. This is why it is so important that we learn to live in our spirit man and to keep constant and consistent fellowship with God. We will win in the final battle if, and only if, we live with the spirit as king and Jesus as Lord. By living in the spirit, we become that triumphant church against which the gates of hell cannot prevail. (Matthew 16:18)

MY CHALLENGE TO YOU

If you are not a Christian, I invite you to receive the hope and peace in your heart that only Jesus gives.

To become a Christian, you must deal with Christ Jesus directly. In a quiet moment, bow your head and talk to Him. In your own words say something like this:

"Dear Lord Jesus, I am a sinner. I believe that you died and rose from the dead to save me from my sins. I want to be with you in heaven forever. God forgive me of all my sins that I have committed against you. I here and now open my heart to you and ask you to come into my heart and life and be my personal Saviour. Amen."

If you say that to Christ and mean it, He will come in instantly. At once you will sense you have been transferred from the devil's dominion to the kingdom of God.

Read I John 1:9 and Colossians 1:13. A wonderful peace and joy will fill your soul.

If you pray a prayer like this, let me hear from you. I will send you a little pamphlet entitled, "So You're Born Again!"

Mail your letter to: **Lester Sumrall, P.O. Box 12, South Bend, IN 46624.**

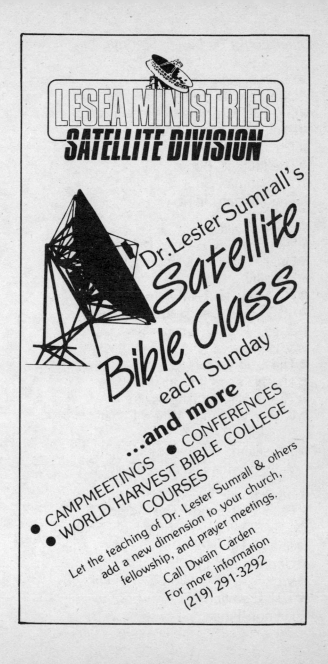

Other books by Lester Sumrall:

LeSEA Publishing Co.
  Dominion Is Yours
● Genesis, Crucible of the Universe
● Paul, Man of the Millennia
  The Total Man
  The Human Body
● The Human Soul
● The Human Spirit

Nelson Publishing Co.
  Demons The Answer Book
  Grief, You Can Conquer It
  Hostility
● My Story To His Glory
  60 Things God Said About Sex
  Supernatural Principalities
  & Powers
  The Cup Of Life
● The Names Of God
● The Reality Of Angels
● Where Was God When Pagan
  Religions Began?
● Jerusalem, Where Empires Die--
  Will America Die At Jerusalem?

Harrison House
  Faith To Change The World
● Gifts & Ministries of the Holy Spirit
● Jihad—The Holy War
● Unprovoked Murder
  Victory & Dominion Over Fear
● 101 Questions & Answers On
  Demon Power